QUIC

FOR YOU

Lion Brand® Homespun®

Made in America in a New Hampshire mill that uses hydro-generated power, Lion Brand Homespun® has long been a favorite of knitters and crocheters. Lovely, lofty and quick to knit or crochet, Homespun is available in dozens of beautifully blended colorways, from heathery tweeds to painterly palettes and makes even the simplest of projects look absolutely stunning. Homespun's bulky weight results in a fast finish for sweaters and afghans and its wash-and-wear care makes it ideal for almost any project.

Lion Brand® Homespun® Thick & Quick®

Make a statement with Homespun® Thick & Quick®. This super-bulky version of our fan-favorite Homespun® yarn works up quickly into richly textured afghans and silky-soft accessories such as hats, scarves and cowls. Made in an American mill in New Hampshire, this beautiful yarn features both heathers and slowly striping painterly shades, so you're sure to find the color you love. This is sure to be your go-to yarn for quick-finish projects.

About Lion Brand® Yarn Company

Lion Brand® Yarn Company is a family-owned and operated business and a beloved American brand since 1878. Throughout its history, Lion Brand Yarn has been at the forefront of yarn trends while consistently providing its customers with the highest quality product at a value price. The company's mission is to provide ideas, inspiration and education to yarn crafters.

LEISURE ARTS, INC.
Maumelle, Arkansas

PONCHO WITH COWL

 **EASY**

SIZE

Finished Length: About 14½" (37 cm), not including cowl
Finished Circumference at Lower Edge: About 79" (200.5 cm)

SHOPPING LIST

Yarn

(Super Bulky Weight) 🧶 **6**
LION BRAND® HOMESPUN® THICK & QUICK® (Art. #792)

☐ #207 Greystone Stripes - 2 skeins (A)
   or color of your choice

(Bulky Weight) 🧶 **5**
LION BRAND® HOMESPUN® (Art. #790)

☐ #411 Mixed Berries - 1 skein (B)
   or color of your choice

Crochet Hooks

LION BRAND® crochet hooks

☐ Size P-15 (10 mm) **and**
☐ Size K-10.5 (6.5 mm)
   or size needed for gauge

Additional Supplies

☐ LION BRAND® large-eyed blunt needle

GAUGE

4 sts = about 5" (12.5 cm) with larger hook and A over pattern; 7½ sc = 4" (10 cm) with smaller hook and B.
BE SURE TO CHECK YOUR GAUGE.

── STITCH GUIDE ──

PICOT
Ch 3, sl st in 3rd ch from hook.
V-STITCH (abbreviated V-st)
2 dc in indicated stitch or space.

─────────────

NOTES
1. Poncho is worked in joined rnds beg at neck.
2. Cowl collar is worked around neck edge of completed Poncho.

PONCHO

With larger hook and A, ch 56; join with sl st in beg ch to form a ring.

Rnd 1: Ch 1, sc in same st as joining and in each ch around; join with sl st in first sc – 56 sc.

Rnd 2: Ch 1, 2 sc in same st as joining, sc in next st , *2 sc in next st, sc in next st; rep from * around; join with sl st in first sc – 84 sts.

Rnd 3: Ch 3 (counts as first dc in this rnd and in all following rnds), dc in each st around; join with sl st in top of beg ch.

Rnd 4: Ch 3, dc in same st as joining (first V-st made), ch 2, sk next st, sc in next st, *ch 2, sk next st, V-st in next st, ch 2, sk next st, sc in next st; rep from * to last st, ch 2, sk last st; join with sl st in top of beg ch – 21 V-sts, 21 sc and 42 ch-2 sps.

Rnd 5: Ch 1, (sc, ch 3, sc) in sp between 2-dc of first V-st, *ch 4, (sc, ch 3, sc) in sp between 2-dc of next V-st; rep from * around, ch 4; join with sl st in first sc – 42 sc, 21 ch-3 sps and 42 ch-4 sps.

Rnd 6: (Sl st, ch 3, dc) in first ch-3 sp (first V-st made), ch 2, sc in next ch-4 sp, *ch 2, V-st in next ch-3 sp, ch 2, sc in next ch-4 sp; rep from * around, ch 2; join with sl st in top of beg ch.

Rnds 7-16: Rep last 2 rnds 5 more times. Fasten off.

FINISHING
EDGING
From RS with smaller hook, join B with sc in any sc along lower edge of Poncho, *picot, sc in next ch-sp, picot, sc in sp between 2 dc of next V-st, picot, sc in next ch-sp, picot, sc in next sc; rep from * around omitting last sc; join with sl st in first sc – 84 picots. Fasten off.

COWL
Rnd 1: From WS with smaller hook, join B with sl st anywhere along neck edge of Poncho. Working along opposite side of foundation ch, ch 1, sc in each ch around; join with sl st in first sc – 56 sts.

Rnds 2-12: Ch 1, sc in each st around; join with sl st in first sc.

Rnd 13: Ch 1, sc in same st as joining, *2 sc in next st, sc in next 10 sts; rep from * 4 more times; join with sl st in first st – 61 sts.

Rnds 14-16: Rep Rnd 2.

Rnd 17: Ch 1, sc in same st as joining, *picot, sc in next 2 sts; rep from * around; join with sl st in first st – 30 picots. Fasten off.

Weave in ends.

TWO-TONE SHAWL

 **INTERMEDIATE +**

SIZE
About 27" x 55" (68.5 cm x 139.5 cm)

SHOPPING LIST

Yarn (Bulky Weight) 🔵**5**
LION BRAND® HOMESPUN® (Art. #790)
- ☐ #602 Blue Moon - 2 skeins (A)
- ☐ #312 Edwardian - 1 skein (B)

  or colors of your choice

Crochet Hook
LION BRAND® crochet hook
- ☐ Size K-10.5 (6.5 mm)

  or size needed for gauge

Additional Supplies
- ☐ LION BRAND® large-eyed blunt needle

GAUGE
11 sts + 4 rows = 4" (10 cm) in pattern.
BE SURE TO CHECK YOUR GAUGE.

—STITCH GUIDE—

BACK POST DOUBLE CROCHET (abbreviated BPDC)
Yarn over, insert hook from back to front then to back, going around post of indicated st, draw up a loop, (yarn over and draw through 2 loops on hook) twice. Sk st in front of the BPDC.

FRONT POST DOUBLE CROCHET (abbreviated FPDC)
Yarn over, insert hook from front to back then to front, going around post of indicated st, draw up a loop, (yarn over and draw through 2 loops on hook) twice. Sk st behind the FPDC.

FRONT POST SINGLE CROCHET (abbreviated FPSC)
Insert hook from front to back then to front, going around post of indicated st, draw up a loop, yarn over and draw through both loops on hook. Skip st behind the FPSC.

LARGE-SHELL (abbreviated lg-shell)
(3 dc, ch 2, 3 dc) in indicated st or ch-sp.

PICOT
Ch 3, sl st in 3rd ch from hook.

SMALL SHELL (abbreviated sm-shell)
(2 dc, ch 2, 2 dc) in indicated ch-sp.

V-STITCH (abbreviated V-st)
(Dc, ch 1, dc) in indicated st or ch-sp.

NOTES
1. Shawl is worked back and forth in rows beg at center back neck.
2. Shawl is worked with 2 colors. To change color, work last st of old color to last yarn over. Yarn over with new color and draw through all loops on hook to complete st. Proceed with new color. Fasten off old color.

SHAWL
With A, ch 5.

Row 1: Lg-shell in 5th ch from hook (beg ch counts as dc, ch 1), ch 1, dc in same ch – 1 lg-shell, 2 ch-1 sps, 1 dc at beg of row, and 1 dc at end of this row.

Row 2: Ch 4 (always counts as dc, ch 1), turn, 3 dc in next ch-1 sp, ch 1, lg-shell in ch-2 sp of center lg-shell, ch 1, 3 dc in beg ch-sp, ch 1, dc in 3rd ch of beg ch – 1 lg-shell, two 3-dc groups, 4 ch-1 sps, 1 dc at beg of row, and 1 dc at end of this row.

Row 3: Ch 4, turn, 3 dc in first ch-1 sp, ch 1, 3-dc in next ch-1 sp, ch 1, lg-shell in ch-2 sp of center lg-shell, ch 1, 3 dc in next ch-1 sp, ch 1, 3 dc in turning ch-sp, ch 1, dc in 3rd ch of turning ch – 1 lg-shell, four 3-dc groups, 6 ch-1 sps, 1 dc at beg of row, and 1 dc at end of this row.

Row 4: Ch 4, turn, 2 dc in first ch-1 sp, dc in each dc and ch-1 sp to center ch-2 sp, sm-shell in center ch-2 sp, dc in each dc and ch-1 sp to turning ch-sp, 2 dc in turning ch-sp, ch 1, dc in 3rd ch of turning ch – 1 sm-shell, 28 dc, and 2 ch-1 sps.

Row 5: Ch 4, turn, 2 dc in first ch-1 sp, FPDC around each dc to center ch-2 sp, sm-shell in center ch-2 sp, FPDC around each dc to turning ch-sp, 2 dc in turning ch-sp, ch 1, dc in 3rd ch of turning ch – 1 sm-shell, 36 dc, and 2 ch-1 sps.

Row 6: Ch 4, turn, 3 dc in first ch-1 sp, *ch 1, sk next 3 sts, 3 dc in next st; rep from * to 3 sts before center ch-2 sp, ch 1, sk next 3 sts, lg-shell in center ch-2 sp, **ch 1, sk next 3 sts, 3 dc in next st; rep from ** to 3 sts before turning ch-sp, ch 1, sk next 3 sts, 3 dc in turning ch-sp, ch 1, dc in 3rd ch of turning ch – 1 lg-shell, ten 3-dc groups,12 ch-1 sps, 1 dc at beg of row, and 1 dc at end of this row.

Row 7: Ch 4, turn, 3 dc in first ch-1 sp, *ch 1, 3 dc in next ch-1 sp; rep from * to center lg-shell, ch 1, lg-shell in ch-2 sp of center lg-shell, **ch 1, 3 dc in next ch-1 sp; rep from ** to turning ch-sp, ch 1, 3 dc in turning ch-sp, ch 1, dc in 3rd ch of turning ch – 1 lg-shell, twelve 3-dc groups, and 14 ch-1 sps.

Rows 8-19: Rep last 4 rows 3 more times – 1 lg-shell, thirty-six 3-dc groups, and 38 ch-1 sps at the end of Row 19.

Rows 20 and 21: Rep Rows 4 and 5 – 1 sm-shell, 164 dc, and 2 ch-1 sps at the end of Row 21. Change to B.

Row 22: Ch 4, turn, 2 dc in first ch-1 sp, *FPDC around next st, dc in next 3 sts, FPDC around next st, sk next st, V-st in next st, sk next st; rep from * to 3 sts before center ch-2 sp, FPDC around next st, dc in next 2 sts, (dc, ch 2, dc) in center ch-2 sp, dc in next 2 sts, FPDC around next st, **sk next st, V-st in next st, sk next st, FPDC around next st, dc in next 3 sts, FPDC around next st; rep from ** to turning ch-sp, 2 dc in turning ch-sp, ch 1, dc in 3rd ch of turning ch – 20 V-sts (10 across each diagonal side edge).

Row 23: Ch 4, turn, 2 dc in first ch-1 sp, dc in next 2 sts, BPDC around next st, *dc in next 3 sts, BPDC around next st, sk next st, V-st in ch-1 sp of next V-st, sk next st, BPDC around next st; rep from * to 3 sts before center ch-2 sp, dc in next 3 sts, (2 dc, ch 1, dc, ch 2, dc, ch 1, 2 dc) in center ch-2 sp, dc in next 3 sts, BPDC around next st, **sk next st, V-st in ch-1 sp of next V-st, sk next st, BPDC around next st, dc in next 3 sts, BPDC around next st; rep from ** to 2 sts before turning ch-sp, dc in next 2 sts, 2 dc in turning ch-sp, ch 1, dc in 3rd ch of turning ch.

Row 24: Ch 4, turn, 2 dc in first ch-1 sp, FPDC around next st, sk next st, V-st in next st, sk next st, *FPDC around next st, dc in next 3 sts, FPDC around next st, sk next st, V-st in next ch-1 sp, sk next st; rep from * to center ch-2 sp, (dc, ch 2, dc) in center ch-2 sp, **sk next st, V-st in next ch-1 sp, sk next st, FPDC around next st, dc in next 3 sts, FPDC around next st; rep from ** to 4 sts before turning ch-sp, sk next st, V-st in next st, sk next st, FPDC around next st, 2 dc in turning ch-sp, ch 1, dc in 3rd ch of turning ch – 24 V-sts (12 across each diagonal side edge).

Row 25: Ch 4, turn, 2 dc in first ch-1 sp, dc in next 2 sts, BPDC around next st, sk next st, V-st in ch-1 sp of next V-st, sk next st, BPDC around next st, *dc in next 3 sts, BPDC around next st, sk next st, V-st in ch-1 sp of next V-st, sk next st, BPDC around next st; rep from * to center ch-2 sp, lg-shell in center ch-2 sp, BPDC around next st, sk next st, V-st in ch-1 sp of next V-st, sk next st, BPDC around next st, **dc in next 3 sts, BPDC around next st, sk next st, V-st in ch-1 sp of next V-st, sk next st, BPDC around next st; rep from ** to 2 sts before turning ch-sp, dc in next 2 sts, 2 dc in turning ch-sp, ch 1, dc in 3rd ch of turning ch.

Row 26: Ch 4, turn, 2 dc in first ch-1 sp, FPDC around next st, dc in next 3 sts, *FPDC around next st, sk next st, (2 dc, ch 1, 2 dc) in ch-1 sp of next V-st, sk next st, FPDC around next st, dc in next 3 sts; rep from * to center ch-2 sp, lg-shell in center ch-2 sp, dc in next 3 sts, FPDC around next st, **sk next st, (2 dc, ch 1, 2 dc) in ch-1 sp of next V-st, sk next st, FPDC around next st, dc in next 3 sts, FPDC around next st; rep from ** to turning ch-sp, 2 dc in turning ch-sp, ch 1, dc in 3rd ch of turning ch.

Rnd 27: Ch 1, turn, sc in first st, picot, sk first ch-1 sp, sc in next 2 sts, FPSC around next st, sc in next 3 sts, FPSC around next st, *sc in next 2 sts, picot, sk next ch-1 sp, sc in next 2 sts, FPSC around next st, sc in next 3 sts, FPSC around next st; rep from * to 2 sts before center ch-2 sp, sc in next 2 sts, picot, sk center ch-2 sp, sc in next 2 sts, FPSC around next st, sc in next 3 sts, FPSC around next st, **sc in next 2 sts, picot, sk next ch-1 sp, sc in next 2 sts, FPSC around next st, sc in next 3 sts, FPSC around next st; rep from ** to 2 sts before turning ch-sp, sc in next 2 sts, picot, sc in 3rd ch of turning ch; working in ends of rows across long straight top edge, work 2 sc in end of each row all the way across; join with sl st in first sc of this rnd. Fasten off.

FINISHING
Weave in ends.

COLLARED CAPELET

SIZE

Finished Circumference: About 50" (127 cm) at lower edge
Finished Length: 20" (51 cm), not including collar

SHOPPING LIST

Yarn (Bulky Weight)
LION BRAND® HOMESPUN® (Art. #790)

☐ #341 Windsor - 3 skeins
or color of your choice

Crochet Hook

LION BRAND® crochet hook

☐ Size K-10.5 (6.5 mm)
or size needed for gauge

Additional Supplies

☐ LION BRAND® large-eyed blunt needle
☐ 2 buttons 1½" (38 mm) diameter
☐ Sewing needle and thread

GAUGE

1 pattern rep + 5½ rows = 4" (10 cm) in pattern of Body.
BE SURE TO CHECK YOUR GAUGE.

Note: One pattern rep consists of one post st and 3 V-sts.

STITCH GUIDE

BACK POST DOUBLE CROCHET (abbreviated BPDC)

Yarn over, insert hook from back to front then to back, going around post of indicated st, draw up a loop, (yarn over and draw through 2 loops on hook) twice. Skip st in front of the BPDC.

BACK POST SINGLE CROCHET (abbreviated BPSC)

Insert hook from back to front then to back again, going around post of indicated st, draw up a loop, yarn over and draw through both loops on hook. Skip st in front of the BPSC.

5 DOUBLE CROCHET CLUSTER (abbreviated Cl)

Yarn over, insert hook in indicated st, yarn over and draw up a loop, yarn over and draw through 2 loops on hook (2 loops rem on hook), (yarn over, insert hook in same st, yarn over and draw up a loop, yarn over and draw through 2 loops on hook) 4 times (6 loops rem on hook) yarn over, draw through all loops on hook.

FRONT POST DOUBLE CROCHET (abbreviated FPDC)

Yarn over, insert hook from front to back then to front, going around post of indicated st, draw up a loop, (yarn over and draw through 2 loops on hook) twice. Skip st behind the FPDC.

FRONT POST SINGLE CROCHET (abbreviated FPSC)

Insert hook from front to back then to front again, going around post of indicated st, draw up a loop, yarn over and draw through both loops on hook. Skip st behind the FPSC.

SHELL

Work (2 dc, ch 1, 2 dc) in indicated sp.

V-STITCH (abbreviated V-st)

Work (dc, ch 1, dc) in indicated st or sp.

NOTES

1. Body of Capelet is worked sideways.
2. Sts for yoke and collar are picked up along one edge of Body.

CAPELET
Body
Ch 40.

Row 1 (RS): Sc in 2nd ch from hook and in each ch across – 39 sc.

Row 2: Ch 1, turn, BPSC around each st across.

Row 3: Ch 3 (counts as first dc in this row and in all following rows), turn, FPDC around next st, dc in next 5 sts, *FPDC around next st, (sk next st, V-st in next st) 3 times, sk next st; rep from * 2 more times, FPDC around next st, dc in next 5 sts, FPDC around next st, dc in last st – 9 V-sts.

Row 4: Ch 3, turn, BPDC around next st, dc in next 5 sts, *BPDC around next st, V-st in ch-1 sp of each of next 3 V-sts; rep from * 2 more times, BPDC around next st, dc in next 5 sts, BPDC around next st, dc in top of turning ch.

Row 5: Ch 3, turn, FPDC around next st, dc in next 2 sts, Cl in next st, dc in next 2 sts, *FPDC around next st, V-st in ch-1 sp of each of next 3 V-sts; rep from * 2 more times, FPDC around next st, dc in next 2 sts, Cl in next st, dc in next 2 sts, FPDC around next st, dc in top of turning ch.

Row 6: Rep Row 4.

Row 7: Ch 3, turn, FPDC around next st, dc in next 5 sts, *FPDC around next st, V-st in ch-1 sp of each of next 3 V-sts; rep from * 2 more times, FPDC around next st, dc in next 5 sts, FPDC around next st, dc in top of turning ch.

Row 8: Ch 1, turn, sc in first st, BPSC around next st, FPSC around each of next 5 sts, *BPSC around next st, (sc, ch 1, sc) in ch-1 sp of each of next 3 V-sts; rep from * 2 more times, BPSC around next st, FPSC around each of next 5 sts, BPSC around next st, sc in top of turning ch.

Row 9: Ch 3, turn, FPDC around next st, dc in next 5 sts, *FPDC around next st, V-st in each of next 3 ch-1 sps (skipping the sc sts on each side of the ch-1 sps); rep from * 2 more times, FPDC around next st, dc in next 5 sts, FPDC around next st, dc in top of turning ch.

Rows 10-63: Rep Rows 4-9 nine times.

Rows 64-67: Rep Rows 4-7.

Row 68: Ch 1, turn, FPSC in each st across. Fasten off.

Yoke

Row 1 (RS): From RS, join yarn with sc in corner of Body to work across a long edge, work 68 sc evenly spaced across edge – 69 sts.

Row 2: Ch 3, turn, *BPDC around next st, dc in next 5 sts; rep from * to last 2 sts, BPDC around next st, dc in last st.

Row 3: Ch 3, turn, *FPDC around next st, dc in next 5 sts; rep from * to last 2 sts, FPDC around next st, dc in top of turning ch.

Row 4: Ch 3, turn, *BPDC around next st, sk next st, dc in next 4 sts; rep from * to last 2 sts, BPDC around next st, dc in top of turning ch – 58 sts.

Row 5: Ch 3, turn, *FPDC around next st, dc in next 4 sts; rep from * to last 2 sts, FPDC around next st, dc in top of turning ch.

Row 6: Ch 3, turn, *BPDC around next st, sk next st, dc in next 3 sts; rep from * to last 2 sts, BPDC around next st, dc in top of turning ch – 47 sts.

Row 7: Ch 3, turn, *FPDC around next st, dc in next 3 sts; rep from * to last 2 sts, FPDC around next st, dc in top of turning ch.

Row 8: Ch 3, turn, *BPDC around next st, sk next st, dc in next 2 sts; rep from * to last 2 sts, BPDC around next st, dc in top of turning ch – 36 sts.

Collar

Note: Row 9 is worked on the RS of the yoke, but because the Collar will be folded over, Row 9 is the WS of the Collar.

Row 9 (WS of Collar): Ch 3, turn, *BPDC around next st, dc in next 2 sts; rep from * to last 2 sts, BPDC around next st, dc in top of turning ch.

Row 10: Ch 3, turn, *FPDC around next st, dc in next 2 sts; rep from * to last 2 sts, FPDC around next st, dc in top of turning ch.

Row 11: Rep Row 9.

Row 12: Ch 3, turn, *FPDC around next st, sk next st, V-st in next st; rep from * to last 2 sts, FPDC around next st, dc in top of turning ch – 11 V-sts.

Row 13: Ch 3, turn, *BPDC around next st, V-st in ch-1 sp of next V-st; rep from * to last 2 sts, BPDC around next st, dc in top of turning ch.

Row 14: Ch 3, turn, FPDC around next st, shell in ch-1 sp of next V-st, *FPDC around next st, V-st in ch-1 sp of next V-st, FPDC around next st, shell in ch-1 sp of next V-st; rep from * to last 2 sts, FPDC around next st, dc in top of turning ch – 6 shells and 5 V-sts.

Row 15: Ch 3, turn, BPDC around next st, shell in ch-1 sp of next shell, *BPDC around next st, V-st in ch-1 sp of next V-st, FPDC around next st, shell in ch-1 sp of next shell; rep from * to last 2 sts, BPDC around next st, dc in top of turning ch.

Row 16: Ch 3, turn, FPDC around next st, shell in ch-1 sp of next shell, *FPDC around next st, V-st in ch-1 sp of next V-st, FPDC around next st, shell in ch-1 sp of next shell; rep from * to last 2 sts, FPDC around next st, dc in top of turning ch. Do not fasten off.

Edging: Do not turn, *ch 3, sc in end of next row or next st; rep from * along both sides and lower edge of piece; working across sts of Row 16, ch 3, sc in first FPDC, ch 3, (sc, ch 3, sc) in ch-1 sp of next shell, ch 3, sc in next FPDC, **ch 3, sc in ch-1 sp of next V-st, ch 3, sc in next FPDC, ch 3, (sc, ch 3, sc) in ch-1 sp of next shell, ch 3, sc in next FPDC; rep from ** across; ch 3; join with sl st in base of beg ch. Fasten off.

FINISHING
With sewing needle and thread, sew buttons to right front. Use sps between sts for buttonholes. Weave in ends.

V-PONCHO

■■□□ EASY

SIZE
Finished Circumference at Lower Edge:
About 76" (193 cm) at lower edge
Finished Length: About 19" (48.5 cm)

SHOPPING LIST

Yarn (Super Bulky Weight)
LION BRAND® HOMESPUN® THICK & QUICK® (Art. #792)

- ☐ #312 Edwardian - 1 skein (A)
- ☐ #302 Colonial - 1 skein (B)
- ☐ #434 Relish - 1 skein (C)

  or colors of your choice

Crochet Hook

LION BRAND® crochet hook

- ☐ Size P-15 (10 mm)

  or size needed for gauge

Additional Supplies

- ☐ LION BRAND® large-eyed blunt needle

GAUGE

6 dc + 3½ rnds = about 4" (10 cm).
BE SURE TO CHECK YOUR GAUGE.

—— STITCH GUIDE ——

FRONT POST SINGLE CROCHET (abbreviated FPSC)
Insert hook from front to back then to front, going around post of indicated st, draw up a loop, yarn over and draw through both loops on hook. Skip st behind the FPSC.

PICOT
Ch 4, sl st in 4th ch from hook.

SHELL
(2 dc, ch 2, 2 dc) in indicated st.

NOTES
1. Poncho is worked in joined rnds, beg at neck edge. Turn at beg of every rnd.
2. Beg after Rnd 5, the color is changed every other rnd. To change color, fasten off old color and draw up a loop of new color in same st as rnd joining.

PONCHO

With A, ch 44; taking care not to twist ch, join with sl st in first ch to form a ring.

Rnd 1 (WS): Ch 1, turn, sc in each ch around; join with sl st in first sc – 44 sc.

Rnd 2: Ch 3 (always counts as first dc), turn, dc in next 7 sc, sk next sc, shell in next sc, (sk next sc, dc in next 8 sc, sk next sc, shell in next sc) 3 times, sk last sc; join with sl st in top of turning ch – 4 shells and 32 dc (8 dc between each shell) at the end of this rnd.

Rnd 3: Ch 3, turn, sk next 2 dc, shell in ch-2 sp, (sk next dc, dc in next 9 dc, sk next 2 dc, shell in ch-2 sp) 3 times, sk next dc, dc in last 8 dc; join with sl st in top of turning ch – 4 shells and 36 dc (9 dc between each shell) at the end of this rnd.

Rnd 4: Ch 3, turn, dc in next 9 dc, sk next dc, shell in ch-2 sp, (sk next 2 dc, dc in next 10 dc, sk next dc, shell in ch-2 sp) 3 times, sk last 2 dc; join with sl st in top of turning ch – 4 shells and 40 dc (10 dc between each shell) at the end of this rnd.

Rnd 5: Ch 1, turn, FPSC around each of next 2 dc, 2 sc in ch-2 sp, (sk next 2 dc, FPSC around each of next 12 dc, 2 sc in ch-2 sp) 3 times, sk next 2 dc, FPSC around each of last 10 dc (the last FPSC is worked around the turning ch); join with sl st in first sc – 56 sts at the end of this rnd. Fasten off.

Rnd 6: From RS, draw up a loop of B in same st as joining leaving a long tail to weave in, ch 3, dc in next 10 sc, sk next sc, shell in next sp between sts, (sk next sc, dc in next 12 sc, sk next sc, shell in next sp between sts) 3 times, sk next sc, dc in last sc; join with sl st in top of turning ch – 4 shells and 48 dc (12 dc between each shell) at the end of this rnd.

Rnd 7: Ch 3, turn, dc in next dc, sk next 2 dc, shell in ch-2 sp, (sk next dc, dc in next 13 dc, sk next 2 dc, shell in ch-2 sp of next shell) 3 times, sk next dc, dc in last 11 dc; join with sl st in top of turning ch – 4 shells and 52 dc (13 dc between each shell) at the end of this rnd. Fasten off.

Rnd 8: With RS facing, draw up a loop of C in same ch as joining leaving a long tail to weave in, ch 3, dc in next 11 dc, sk next 2 dc, shell in ch-2 sp of next shell, (sk next dc, dc in next 14 dc, sk next 2 dc, shell in ch-2 sp of next shell) 3 times, sk next dc, dc in last 2 dc; join with sl st in top of turning ch – 4 shells and 56 dc (14 dc between each shell) at the end of this rnd.

Rnd 9: Ch 1, turn, FPSC around each of next 3 dc, sk next dc, 2 sc in ch-2 sp of next shell, (FPSC around each of next 17 dc, sk next dc, 2 sc in ch-2 sp of next shell) 3 times, FPSC around each of last 14 dc (the last FPSC is worked around the turning ch); join with sl st in first sc – 80 sts at the end of this rnd. Fasten off.

Rnd 10: From RS, draw up a loop of A in same st as joining leaving a long tail to weave in, ch 3, dc in next 14 sc, sk next sc, shell in next sp between sts, (sk next 2 sc, dc in next 16 sc, sk next sc, shell in next sp between sts) 3 times, sk next 2 sc, dc in last sc; join with sl st in top of turning ch – 4 shells and 64 dc (16 dc bet each shell) at the end of this rnd.

Rnd 11: Ch 3, turn, dc in next dc, sk next 2 dc, shell in ch-2 sp of next shell, (sk next dc, dc in next 17 dc, sk next 2 dc, shell in ch-2 sp of next shell) 3 times, sk next dc, dc in last 15 dc; join with sl st in top of turning ch – 4 shells and 68 dc (17 dc between each shell) at the end of this rnd. Fasten off.

Rnd 12: With RS facing, draw up a loop of B in same ch as joining and leaving a long tail to weave in, ch 3, dc in next 15 dc, sk next 2 dc, shell in ch-2 sp of next shell, (sk next dc, dc in next 18 dc, sk next 2 dc, shell in ch-2 sp of next shell) 3 times, sk next dc, dc in last 2 dc; join with sl st in top of turning ch – 4 shells and 72 dc (18 dc between each shell) at the end of this rnd.

Rnd 13: Ch 1, turn, FPSC around each of next 3 dc, sk next sc, 2 sc in ch-2 sp of next shell, (FPSC around each of next 21 dc, sk next sc, 2 sc in ch-2 sp of next shell) 3 times, FPSC around each of last 18 dc (the last FPSC is worked around the turning ch); join with sl st in first sc – 80 sts at the end of this rnd. Fasten off.

Rnd 14: With RS facing, draw up a loop of C in same st as joining leaving a long tail to weave in, ch 3, dc in next 17 sc, sk next 2 sc, shell in next sp between sts, (sk next sc, dc in next 20 sc, sk next 2 sc, shell in next sp between sts) 3 times, sk next sc, dc in last 2 sc; join with sl st in top of turning ch – 4 shells and 80 dc (20 dc between each shell) at the end of this rnd.

Rnd 15: Ch 3, turn, dc in next 2 dc, sk next 2 dc, shell in ch-2 sp of next shell, (sk next dc, dc in next 21 dc, sk next 2 dc, shell in ch-2 sp of next shell) 3 times, sk next dc, dc in last 18 dc; join with sl st in top of turning ch – 4 shells and 84 dc (21 dc between each shell) at the end of this rnd. Fasten off.

Rnd 16: With RS facing, draw up a loop of A in same ch as joining leaving a long tail to weave in, ch 3, dc in next 18 dc, sk next 2 dc, shell in ch-2 sp of next shell, (sk next dc, dc in next 22 dc, sk next 2 dc, shell in ch-2 sp of next shell) 3 times, sk next dc, dc in last 3 dc; join with sl st in top of turning ch – 4 shells and 88 dc (22 dc between each shell) at the end of this rnd.

Rnd 17: Ch 1, turn, (FPSC around each of next 2 dc, picot) twice, FPSC around next dc, (sc, picot, sc) in ch-2 sp of next shell, FPSC around next dc, picot, *(FPSC around each of next 2 dc, picot) 12 times, FPSC around next dc, (sc, picot, sc) in ch-2 sp of next shell, FPSC around next dc, picot; rep from * around to last 19 dc, (FPSC around each of next 2 dc, picot) 9 times, FPSC around each of last 2 dc (last dc in turning ch), picot; join with sl st in first sc. Fasten off.

FINISHING

Tie: With 1 strand each of B and C held tog, make a ch about 60" (152.5 cm) long. Do not fasten off. Remove loop from hook and place on stitch marker to ensure that it does not unravel. Weave ch through sps between sts around neck edge of Poncho, beg and ending at front.

Bobbles on ends of Tie

First Bobble: Return dropped loop to hook, yarn over, insert hook in 3rd ch from hook and draw up a loop (3 loops on hook), (yarn over, insert hook in same ch and draw up a loop) 3 times (9 loops on hook), yarn over and draw through all 9 loops on hook, ch 1, sk 2 ch, sl st in next ch. Fasten off.

Second Bobble: With 1 strand each of B and C held tog, draw up a loop in other end of Tie, work same as first bobble.

Weave in ends.

HOODED SHAWL

■■□□ EASY

SIZE

About 14" x 60" (35.5 cm x 152.5 cm), not including hood

SHOPPING LIST

Yarn (Bulky Weight)
LION BRAND® HOMESPUN® (Art. #790)

- ☐ #605 Sand Dune - 1 skein (A)
- ☐ #602 Blue Moon - 1 skein (B)
- ☐ #600 Clouds - 1 skein (C)
- ☐ #604 Forest - 1 skein (D)
  or colors of your choice

Crochet Hook

LION BRAND® crochet hook

- ☐ Size K-10.5 (6.5 mm)
  or size needed for gauge

Additional Supplies

- ☐ LION BRAND® stitch markers
- ☐ LION BRAND® large-eyed blunt needle

GAUGE

10 sts + 7 rows = 4" (10 cm) in pattern.
BE SURE TO CHECK YOUR GAUGE

STITCH GUIDE

CROSSED DC
(abbreviated cross-dc)
Sk next st, dc in next st, dc in skipped st.

10 DOUBLE CROCHET CLUSTER
(abbreviated Bobble)
Yarn over, insert hook in indicated st, yarn over and draw up a loop, yarn over and draw through 2 loops on hook (2 loops rem on hook), (yarn over, insert hook in same st, yarn over and draw up a loop, yarn over and draw through 2 loops on hook) 9 times (11 loops rem on hook) yarn over, draw through all loops on hook.

NOTES
1. Shawl is worked first, then hood is worked beg across one long edge of Shawl.
2. The last row of the hood is crocheted together, then a long ch and Bobble are worked as trim.
3. Before beg, cut a 5 yd. (4.5 m) length of A and set aside for hood Bobble.
4. To change color, work last st of old color to last yarn over. Yarn over with new color and draw through all loops on hook to complete the st. Continue with new color. Fasten off old color.

SHAWL
With A, ch 37.

Row 1 (RS): Sc in 2nd ch from hook and in each ch across – 36 sc.

Row 2: Ch 3 (counts as first dc in this row and in all following rows), turn, dc in next st, *cross-dc; rep from * to last 2 sts, dc in last 2 sts – 16 cross-dc.

Row 3: Ch 1, turn, sc in each st across.

Row 4: Ch 3, turn, dc in next st, *cross-dc; rep from * to last 2 sts, dc in last 2 sts.

Rows 5-16: Rep Rows 3 and 4 six more times. Change to B.

Rows 17-32: With B, rep Rows 3 and 4 eight times. Change to C.

Rows 33-52: With C, rep Rows 3 and 4 ten times. Change to B.

Rows 53-72: With B, rep Rows 3 and 4 ten times. Change to C.

Rows 73-88: With C, rep Rows 3 and 4 eight times. Change to D.

Rows 89-104: With D, rep Rows 3 and 4 eight times.

Row 105: With D, rep Row 3.

Row 106: Ch 1, turn, sl st in each st across. Fasten off.

Hood
Place 2 markers on one long side of Shawl, each about 18" (45.5 cm) from a corner.

Row 1 (RS): From RS, join D with sl st at first marker, ch 1, work 58 sc evenly spaced across edge to next marker.

Row 2: Ch 3 (counts as first dc), turn, dc in next st, *cross-dc; rep from * to last 2 sts, dc in last 2 sts – 27 cross-dc.

Row 3: Ch 1, turn, sc in each st across.

Row 4: Ch 3, turn, dc in next st, *cross-dc; rep from * to last 2 sts, dc in last 2 sts.

Rows 5-16: Rep Rows 3 and 4 six more times. Change to A.

Rows 17-24: With A, rep Rows 3 and 4 four times.

Joining Row: Fold last row of hood in half; working through both thicknesses, sc in each st across to join top of hood. With 2 strands of A held tog (working yarn + 5 yd. (4.5 m) length of A set aside earlier), ch 14, work Bobble in 4th ch from hook. Fasten off.

FINISHING

BOBBLES (make 6 – 1 each of A and D, and 2 each of B and C)

Note: To work with 2 strands of each color held tog, cut 5 yd. (4.5 m) lengths of each before beginning.

With 2 strands of yarn held tog, ch 4, Bobble in 4th ch from hook. Fasten off.

Tie

With 2 strands of A held tog, make a ch about 45" (114.5 cm) long. Fasten off. Weave tie through sts of Row 1 of hood (at neck).

Sew a Bobble to each end of tie and to each corner of Shawl.

Weave in ends.

BORDERED COWL

■■□□ EASY

SIZE
About 7½" x 43" (19 cm x 109 cm)

GAUGE
11 sts + 5 rows = 4" (10 cm) in pattern.
BE SURE TO CHECK YOUR GAUGE.

—— STITCH GUIDE ——

BACK POST DOUBLE CROCHET (abbreviated BPDC)

Yarn over, insert hook from back to front then to back, going around post of indicated st, draw up a loop, (yarn over and draw through 2 loops on hook) twice. Sk st in front of the BPDC.

FRONT POST DOUBLE CROCHET (abbreviated FPDC)

Yarn over, insert hook from front to back then to front, going around post of indicated st, draw up a loop, (yarn over and draw through 2 loops on hook) twice. Sk st behind the FPDC.

SHELL

(2 dc, ch 2, 2 dc) in indicated st or ch-sp.

NOTES

1. Cowl is worked in two Halves.
2. The First Half is worked back and forth in rows. The short edges are then joined to form a tube.
3. The Second Half is worked in joined rnds beg around one edge of the tube.

COWL
First Half

With A, ch 13.

Row 1 (RS): Dc in 4th ch from hook (beg ch counts as first dc), sk next ch, shell in next ch, sk next ch, dc in next ch, sk next ch, shell in next ch, sk next ch, dc in last 2 ch – 2 shells and 5 dc.

Row 2: Ch 3 (counts as first dc in this row and in all following rows), turn, *BPDC around next st, shell in ch-2 sp of next shell, sk last 2 dc of same shell; rep from * once more, BPDC around next st, dc in top of beg ch – 2 dc, 2 shells, and 3 post sts at the end of this row.

Row 3: Ch 3, turn, *FPDC around next st, shell in ch-2 sp of next shell, sk last 2 dc of same shell; rep from * once more, FPDC around next st, dc in top of beg ch.

Rep last 2 rows until piece measures about 43" (109 cm) from beg. End with a WS row as your last row. Do not fasten off.

Joining Row: Turn, fold piece in half, matching sts of last and first rows; working through both thicknesses, sl st in each st across to join piece into a tube. Fasten off.

Second Half

Rnd 1 (RS): From RS and working in ends of rows across one long edge of First Half, join B with sl st in end of any row, ch 3 (counts as dc in this rnd and in all following rnds), shell in end of next row, *dc in end of next row, shell in end of next row; rep from * around; join with sl st in top of beg ch.

Rnds 2-4: Ch 3, turn, shell in ch-2 sp of next shell, sk last 2 dc of same shell, *FPDC around next st, shell in ch-2 sp of next shell, sk last 2 dc of same shell; rep from * around; join with sl st in top of beg ch. Fasten off.

FINISHING

Weave in ends.

INFINITY COWL

EASY

SIZE
About 7" x 66" (18 cm x 167.5 cm)

SHOPPING LIST

Yarn (Super Bulky Weight)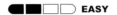
LION BRAND® HOMESPUN® THICK & QUICK® (Art. #792)
- ☐ #315 Tudor - 1 skein (A)
- ☐ #407 Painted Desert - 1 skein (B)
- **or** colors of your choice

Crochet Hook
LION BRAND® crochet hook
- ☐ Size P-15 (10 mm)
- **or** size needed for gauge

Additional Supplies
- ☐ LION BRAND® large-eyed blunt needle

GAUGE
8 sts + 6 rows = about 4" (10 cm) in pattern.
BE SURE TO CHECK YOUR GAUGE.

NOTES

1. Cowl is crocheted back and forth in rows, then ends are joined together to make a tube.
2. Color is changed once. To change color, work last st of old color to last yarn over. Yarn over with new color and draw through all loops on hook to complete st. Proceed with new color. Fasten off old color.

COWL

With A, ch 15.

Row 1: Sc in 3rd ch from hook (skipped chs count as ch-sp), *ch 1, sk next ch, sc in next ch; rep from * across – 7 sc and 7 ch-sps at the end of this row.

Row 2: Ch 2 (counts as ch-sp), turn, sc in first ch-1 sp, *ch 1, sk next sc, sc in next ch-1 sp; rep from * to last sc, ch 1, sk last sc, sc in beg ch-sp.

Rep Row 2 until piece measures about 33" (84 cm) from beg. Change to B.

With B, rep Row 2 until piece measures about 66" (167.5 cm) from beg.

Fasten off. Cut yarn, leaving a long yarn tail.

FINISHING

Hold ends of piece together and join by working sl st through both layers. Fasten off.

Weave in ends.

FRESH AIR BERET & SCARF SET

EASY

SIZE
Beret
Finished circumference: About 20" (51 cm)
Scarf
About 6" x 54" (15 cm x 137 cm)

SHOPPING LIST

Yarn (Super Bulky Weight)
LION BRAND® HOMESPUN® THICK & QUICK® (Art. #792)
- [ ] #329 Waterfall - 1 skein
  or color of your choice

Crochet hook
LION BRAND® crochet hook
- [ ] Size N-13 (9 mm)
  or size needed for gauge

Additional Supplies
- [ ] LION BRAND® large-eyed blunt needle

GAUGE
6 sts + 4 rows = about 4" (10 cm) in pattern.
BE SURE TO CHECK YOUR GAUGE.

─── STITCH GUIDE ───

FRONT POST SINGLE CROCHET (abbreviated FPSC)

Insert hook from front to back then to front, going around post of indicated st, draw up a loop, yarn over and draw through both loops on hook. Skip st behind the FPSC.

NOTES

1. Beret is worked in joined rnds from top of Beret.
2. Scarf is worked back and forth in rows.

BERET

Note: Do not turn at ends of rnds.

Ch 3.

Rnd 1: Work 10 sc in 3rd ch from hook; join with sl st in first sc.

Rnd 2: Ch 4 (counts as dc, ch 1), *dc in next st, ch 1; rep from * around; join with sl st in 3rd ch of beg ch – 10 dc and 10 ch-1 sps at the end of this rnd.

Rnd 3: Sl st in first ch-1 sp, ch 2 (counts as first hdc in this rnd and in all following rnds), hdc in same ch-1 sp, ch 1, *2 hdc in next ch-1 sp, ch 1; rep from * around; join with sl st in top of beg ch – 20 hdc and 10 ch-1 sps.

Rnd 4: Sl st in next hdc, ch 2, 2 hdc in next ch-1 sp, ch 1, *sk next hdc, hdc in next hdc, 2 hdc in next ch-1 sp, ch 1; rep from * around; join with sl st in top of beg ch – 30 hdc and 10 ch-1 sps.

Rnd 5: Sl st in next hdc, ch 2, hdc in next hdc, 2 hdc in next ch-1 sp, ch 1, *sk next hdc, hdc in next 2 hdc, 2 hdc in next ch-1 sp, ch 1; rep from * around; join with sl st in top of beg ch – 40 hdc and 10 ch-1 sps.

Rnd 6: Sl st in next hdc, ch 2, hdc in next 2 hdc, 2 hdc in next ch-1 sp, ch 1, *sk next hdc, hdc in next 3 hdc, 2 hdc in next ch-1 sp, ch 1; rep from * around; join with sl st in top of beg ch – 50 hdc and 10 ch-1 sps.

Rnd 7: Ch 2, hdc in next 4 hdc, ch 1, sk next ch-1 sp, *hdc in next 5 hdc, ch 1, sk next ch-1 sp; rep from * around; join with sl st in top of beg ch.

Rnd 8 (Decrease Rnd): Sl st in next hdc, ch 2, hdc in next 3 hdc, ch 1, sk next ch-1 sp, *sk next hdc, hdc in next 4 hdc, ch 1, sk next ch-1 sp; rep from * around; join with sl st in top of beg ch – 40 hdc and 10 ch-1 sps.

Rnd 9 (Decrease Rnd): Sl st in next hdc, ch 2, hdc in next 2 hdc, ch 1, sk next ch-1 sp,*sk next hdc, hdc in next 3 hdc, ch 1, sk next ch-1 sp; rep from * around; join with sl st in top of beg ch – 30 hdc and 10 ch-1 sps.

Rnd 10 (Decrease Rnd): Sl st in next hdc, ch 2, hdc in next hdc, ch 1, sk next ch-1 sp, *sk next hdc, hdc in next 2 hdc, ch 1, sk next ch-1 sp; rep from * around; join with sl st in top of beg ch – 20 hdc and 10 ch-1 sps.

Note: In following rnds, work first st in same st as joining.

Rnds 11-14: Ch 1, *sc in next 2 sts, FPSC around next st; rep from * around; join with sl st in first sc – 30 sts. Fasten off.

SCARF
Ch 14.

Row 1: Hdc in 4th ch from hook (beg ch counts as hdc, ch 1), *ch 1, sk next ch, hdc in next ch; rep from * across – 7 hdc and 6 ch-1 sps.

Row 2: Ch 3 (counts as hdc, ch 1), turn, hdc in first ch-1 sp, *ch 1, sk next hdc, hdc in next ch-1 sp; rep from * across working last hdc in turning ch-sp.

Rep Row 2 until almost all yarn has been used. Fasten off.

FINISHING
Weave in ends.

SIMPLE CROCHET COWL

⬤▢▢▢ BEGINNER

SIZE
Finished Circumference: About 33" (84 cm)
Finished Height: About 13" (33 cm)

SHOPPING LIST

Yarn (Super Bulky Weight)
LION BRAND® HOMESPUN® THICK & QUICK® (Art. #792)

☐ #412 Pearls - 2 skeins

or color of your choice

Crochet Hook
LION BRAND® crochet hook

☐ Size N-13 (9 mm)

or size needed for gauge

Additional Supplies

☐ LION BRAND® large-eyed blunt needle

GAUGE
8 single crochet = 4" (10 cm).
BE SURE TO CHECK YOUR GAUGE.

COWL

Chain 27.

Row 1: Single crochet in 2nd chain from hook and in each chain across – 26 single crochet.

Row 2: Chain 1, turn, working in back loops only, single crochet in each single crochet across.

Repeat Row 2 until piece measures about 33" (84 cm) from beginning. Do not fasten off. Fold piece in half, matching last row to first row.

Joining Row: Working through both layers, slip stitch in each stitch across to join piece into a ring. Fasten off.

Note: If you prefer, you can sew ends of piece together.

FINISHING

Weave in ends.

DRAWSTRING COWL/HOOD

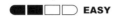 **EASY**

SIZE
Finished Circumference: About 24" (61 cm)
Finished Height: About 19" (48.5 cm)

SHOPPING LIST

Yarn (Bulky Weight) 🧶**5**
LION BRAND® HOMESPUN® (Art # 790)
☐ #408 Wild Fire - 2 skeins
   or color of your choice

Crochet Hook
LION BRAND® crochet hook
☐ Size K-10.5 (6.5 mm)
   or size needed for gauge

Additional Supplies
☐ LION BRAND® large-eyed blunt needle

GAUGE
10 sc = 4" (10 cm).
BE SURE TO CHECK YOUR GAUGE.

NOTES

1. Hood is worked in joined rnds. At the end of each rnd, join last st with sl st in first st. Turn work at the beg of each rnd.

2. If you find it difficult to join the beg ch into a ring without twisting the ch, Rnd 1 can be worked as a row, then joined into a rnd, as follows: Leaving a long beg tail, ch 61, sc in 2nd ch from hook and in each ch across; join with sl st in first sc – 60 sc. Use beg tail to sew gap at base of first row closed. Proceed to Rnd 2.

3. Drawstring is worked first.

DRAWSTRING

Make a chain about 36" (91.5 cm) long.

Row 1: Sl st in 2nd ch from hook and in each ch across. Fasten off.

Hood

Ch 60; taking care not to twist the ch; join with sl st in first ch to form a ring.

Rnd 1: Ch 1, sc in same ch as joining and in each ch around; join with sl st in first sc – 60 sts at the end of this rnd.

Rnd 2: Ch 3 (counts as first dc in this rnd and in all following rnds), turn, dc in each sc around; join with sl st in top of turning ch.

Rnd 3: Ch 1, turn, sc in each dc around; join with sl st in first sc.

Repeat Rnds 2 and 3 until piece measures about 19" (48.5 cm) from beg. Fasten off.

FINISHING

Weave in ends. Weave Drawstring through Hood, about 5" (12.5 cm) below top edge, weaving in and out about every 1" (2.5 cm).

HOODED COWL

Shown on page 45.

 **EASY**

SIZE

Finished Cowl Circumference: About 22" (56 cm)
Finished Height: About 15½" (39.5 cm) from
lower edge of Cowl to top of Hood

SHOPPING LIST

Yarn (Bulky Weight) **5 BULKY**
LION BRAND® HOMESPUN® (Art # 790)
☐ #404 Lagoon - 1 skein
  or color of your choice

Crochet Hook
LION BRAND® crochet hook
☐ Size K-10.5 (6.5 mm)
  or size needed for gauge

Additional Supplies
☐ LION BRAND® large-eyed blunt needle

GAUGE
9 hdc + 7 rows = about 4" (10 cm).
BE SURE TO CHECK YOUR GAUGE.

— STITCH GUIDE —

**HDC 3 TOGETHER
(abbreviated hdc3tog)**
(Yarn over, insert hook in next st and draw up a loop) 3 times, yarn over and draw through all 7 loops on hook – 2 sts decreased.

NOTES
1. Cowl is worked in joined rnds with RS facing at all times.
2. Hood is worked back and forth in rows over a portion of the sts in the last rnd of Cowl. Last row of Hood is folded and slip stitched to make the top seam.
3. Edging is worked around the entire front opening edge.

HOODED COWL
Cowl
Ch 50; taking care not to twist the ch, join with sl st in first ch to form a ring.

Rnd 1 (RS): Ch 2 (does not count as a st on this rnd or on any of the following rnds), hdc in same ch as joining and in each ch around; join with sl st in top of beg ch – 50 sts.

Rnd 2: Ch 2, hdc in same st and in each st around; join with sl st in top of beg ch.

Repeat Rnd 2 until piece measures about 6" (15 cm) from beg.

Hood
Row 1 (RS): Ch 2, do not turn, hdc in first 33 sts; leave rem sts unworked.

Row 2: Ch 2, turn, hdc in first 4 sts, 2 hdc in next st, (hdc in next 2 sts, 2 hdc in next st) 3 times, hdc in next 5 sts, 2 hdc in next st, (hdc in next 2 sts, 2 hdc in next st) 3 times, hdc in next 4 sts – 41 sts at the end of this row.

Rows 3-14: Ch 2, turn, hdc in each st across.

SHAPE HOOD
Row 15: Ch 2, turn, hdc in next 19 sts, hdc3tog, hdc in next 19 sts – 39 sts.

Row 16: Ch 2, turn, hdc in next 18 sts, hdc3tog, hdc in next 18 sts – 37 sts.

Row 17: Ch 2, turn, hdc in next 17 sts, hdc3tog, hdc in next 17 sts – 35 sts.

Top Seam: Fold Hood in half, bringing RS together. From WS and working through both thicknesses, sl st in each st across. Fasten off.

FINISHING
FRONT EDGING

Note: Before working edging, try piece on and decide whether you'd like to change the size of the face opening.

To reduce the size of the face opening, work fewer sc sts in Rnd 1. To enlarge the size of the face opening, work more sc sts in Rnd 1.

Rnd 1: From RS, join yarn with sl st anywhere in edge of face opening, sc evenly around entire edge of opening; join with sl st in first sc.

Rnd 2: Ch 1, sc in each st around; join with sl st in first sc. Fasten off.

Weave in ends.

GENERAL INSTRUCTIONS

ABBREVIATIONS

beg = begin(ning)(s)
ch = chain
ch-sp(s) = chain space(s)
    previously made
cm = centimeter
hdc = half double crochet
dc = double crochet
hdc = half double crochet
mm = millimeters
rep = repeat
RS = right side
rnd(s) = round(s)
sc = single crochet
sk = skip
sl st = slip stitch
sp(s) = space(s)
st(s) = stitch(es)
tog = together
tr = treble (triple) crochet
WS = wrong side

* — When you see an asterisk used within a pattern row, the symbol indicates that later you will be told to repeat a portion of the instruction. Most often the instructions will say, repeat from * so many times.

( ) or [ ] — Set off a short number of stitches that are repeated or indicate additional information.

— When you see – followed by a number of stitches, this tells you how many stitches you will have at the end of a row or round.

GAUGE

Never underestimate the importance of gauge. Achieving the correct gauge assures that the finished size of your piece matches the finished size given in the pattern.

CROCHET TERMINOLOGY

UNITED STATES		INTERNATIONAL
slip stitch (slip st)	=	single crochet (sc)
single crochet (sc)	=	double crochet (dc)
half double crochet (hdc)	=	half treble crochet (htr)
double crochet (dc)	=	treble crochet(tr)
treble crochet (tr)	=	double treble crochet (dtr)
double treble crochet (dtr)	=	triple treble crochet (ttr)
triple treble crochet (tr tr)	=	quadruple treble crochet (qtr)
skip	=	miss

Yarn Weight Symbol & Names	LACE (0)	SUPER FINE (1)	FINE (2)	LIGHT (3)	MEDIUM (4)	BULKY (5)	SUPER BULKY (6)
Type of Yarns in Category	Fingering, 10-count crochet thread	Sock, Fingering Baby	Sport, Baby	DK, Light Worsted	Worsted, Afghan, Aran	Chunky, Craft, Rug	Bulky, Roving
Crochet Gauge* Ranges in Single Crochet to 4" (10 cm)	32-42 double crochets**	21-32 sts	16-20 sts	12-17 sts	11-14 sts	8-11 sts	5-9 sts
Advised Hook Size Range	Steel*** 6,7,8 Regular hook B-1	B-1 to E-4	E-4 to 7	7 to I-9	I-9 to K-10.5	K-10.5 to M-13	M-13 and larger

*GUIDELINES ONLY: The chart above reflects the most commonly used gauges and hook sizes for specific yarn categories.

** Lace weight yarns are usually crocheted on larger-size hooks to create lacy openwork patterns. Accordingly, a gauge range is difficult to determine. Always follow the gauge stated in your pattern.

*** Steel crochet hooks are sized differently from regular hooks–the higher the number the smaller the hook, which is the reverse of regular hook sizing.

◼◻◻◻ BEGINNER	Projects for first-time crocheters using basic stitches. Minimal shaping.
◼◼◻◻ EASY	Projects using yarn with basic stitches, repetitive stitch patterns, simple color changes, and simple shaping and finishing.
◼◼◼◻ INTERMEDIATE	Projects using a variety of techniques, such as basic lace patterns or color patterns, mid-level shaping and finishing.
◼◼◼◼ EXPERIENCED	Projects with intricate stitch patterns, techniques and dimension, such as non-repeating patterns, multi-color techniques, fine threads, small hooks, detailed shaping and refined finishing.

CROCHET HOOKS															
U.S.	B-1	C-2	D-3	E-4	F-5	G-6	H-8	I-9	J-10	K-10½	L-11	M/N-13	N/P-15	P/Q	Q	S
Metric - mm	2.25	2.75	3.25	3.5	3.75	4	5	5.5	6	6.5	8	9	10	15	16	19

CHECKING YOUR GAUGE

Work a swatch that is at least 4" (10 cm) square. Use the suggested hook size and the number of stitches given. If your swatch is larger than 4" (10 cm), you need to work it again using a smaller hook; if it is smaller than 4" (10 cm), try it with a larger hook. This might require a swatch or two to get the exact gauge given in the pattern.

METRICS

As a handy reference, keep in mind that 1 ounce = approximately 28 grams and 1" = 2.5 centimeters.

TERMS

continue in this way or as established — Once a pattern is set up (established), the instructions may tell you to continue in the same way.

fasten off — To end your piece, you need to simply cut the yarn, then pull the yarn tail through the last loop left on the hook. This keeps the last stitch intact and prevents the work from unraveling.

right side — Refers to the front of the piece.

VISIT LionBrand.com FOR:

- Learn to Knit & Crochet Instructions
- Weekly newsletter with articles, tips, and updates
- Store Locator